Contents

Parties 2

A festival in Brazil 4

New Year 6

Chinese New Year 8

Diwali 12

Glossary 16

PARTIES

Some days are important to us.

People like to have a party on important days.

We can have parties in lots of places. We can have a party at home. We can have a party in the street.

Festivals take place on very important days. A festival is like a very big party. This festival takes place in Brazil.

The festival in Brazil has a big parade. People like to dance in the parade. They like to dance the Samba!

NEW YEAR

Many people like to have a party on New Year's Eve.
They like to sing and dance.

At midnight, people like to sing.

New Year's Eve is very important in Scotland.
In Scotland, a piper pipes in the new year at midnight.

He plays his bagpipes to pipe in the new year.

CHINESE NEW YEAR

Chinese people like to have a party at Chinese New Year. Chinese New Year is a very important festival.

The Chinese New Year festival can last for fifteen days!

At Chinese New Year, people dress up as lions and dragons. The lions and dragons dance in the streets.

People like to watch them dance.

Chinese people like to put up decorations at New Year.
Lots of the decorations are red and gold.

Chinese people say red and gold decorations are lucky.

At Chinese New Year, people give children lucky money.
The lucky money is put into red envelopes.

Children like to get lots of red envelopes!

DIWALI

Indian people have a festival called Diwali. Diwali takes place in October or November.

Diwali is a festival of lights. Indian temples have lots of lights in them at Diwali.

Indian people put lots of lamps in the temple for Diwali.
The lamps are lit one at a time.

Indian people have lots of fireworks, too.
The children like to see the fireworks at Diwali.

Glossary

dance

decorations

dragon

festival

fireworks

lamps

lion

midnight

money

parade

party

temple